DATE DUE			

The First Supersonic Flight

Captain Charles E. Yeager Breaks the Sound Barrier

The First Supersonic Flight

Captain Charles E. Yeager Breaks the Sound Barrier

by Richard L. Taylor

Franklin Watts
New York / Chicago / London / Toronto / Sydney
A First Book

Cover photographs copyright ©: Tony Stone, Inc./Mitsuo Shishido; The Cradle of Aviation Museum (inset); Photographs copyright ©: Wide World Photos: pp. 6, 12, 14, 15, 24, 25, 30, 34, 35, 51 inset; North Wind Picture Archives, Alfred, Me.: pp. 10, 11; The Smithsonian Institution: pp. 10 inset, 17, 22, 33, 38; The Cradle of Aviation Museum: pp. 20, 44, 46, 53, 57; Comstock, Inc./Mike & Carol Werner: p. 29; UPI/Bettmann: pp. 42, 55, 60; Museum of Flight, Photographic Collection, Seattle, Wa.: pp. 50, 51; Jay Mallin: p. 56.

Library of Congress Cataloging-in-Publication Data
Taylor, Richard L.
The first supersonic flight: Captain Charles E. Yeager breaks the sound
barrier / Richard L. Taylor
p. cm — (First book)
Includes bibliographical references and index.
ISBN 0-531-20177-5
1. High-speed aeronautics—History—Juvenile literature. 2. Airplanes—United States—
Speed records—Juvenile literature. 3. Bell X-1 (Supersonic planes)—Juvenile literature.
4. Yeager, Chuck, 1923– —Juvenile literature. [1. High-speed aeronautics—History.
2. Airplanes—Speed records. 3. Bell X-1 (Supersonic planes). 4. Yeager, Chuck,
1923– .] I. Title. II. Series.
TL551.5T39 1994
629.13'09—dc20   94-57   CIP   AC

Contents

Breaking the Sound Barrier

Ka-boom! A thunderclap broke the silence of California's Mojave Desert on an October morning in 1947. But there were no storms to be seen, and the sound wasn't natural thunder, it was man-made thunder—the first time that an airplane had caused a sonic boom.

High above the desert, 13 miles (21 km) above the sand and the sagebrush and the Joshua trees, the Bell X-1, a tiny, experimental airplane, had flown faster than the speed of sound. The shock waves it generated bounced off the earth, making a noise like thunder. The sonic boom, as it was soon named, became the signature of any flight that exceeds the speed of sound. The energy in these shock waves is great enough to cause damage to buildings and discomfort to people, and today pilots are not permitted to fly that fast over the United States. But, in 1947, the sonic boom was welcomed as a signal that a long program of test flights had succeeded—Captain Charles Yeager had become the first human being to fly faster than the speed of sound.

The Problems of High-Speed Flight

Forty years earlier, the Wright brothers were struggling toward a goal of flying at 40 miles (64 km) per hour, the airspeed required by the U.S. government before it would buy airplanes from the Wrights. At that point in the development of aviation, engines weren't powerful enough to move airplanes through the air very fast. But when airplanes began to be used as fighters in World War I, speed became very important, and more-powerful engines were produced.

By the end of World War II, fighter planes were capable of flying at about 400 miles (644 km) per hour, and some adventurous pilots tried to go even faster by diving their airplanes at full power. They discovered that when the airspeed reached a certain point, the airplane would go no faster. There was some sort of barrier that even the most powerful engines could not overcome.

That barrier—whatever it was—might have been

The capabilities and outward appearance of airplanes have changed tremendously since this early model was designed by the Wright brothers (left) in 1903.

accepted as the upper limit of airplane speed if there had not been a remarkable development in power plants. The jet engine became a reality in the early 1940s, and aircraft designers knew that jet-powered airplanes would soon be capable of flying much faster. The mysterious barrier had to be identified, and the problems of flying through it and beyond had to be solved.

Now the battle against the barrier was in the hands of scientists and engineers. They discovered that the problems began to show up as an airplane approached the speed at which sound waves travel through the air.

If sound waves could be seen, they'd look very much like the ripples that spread outward in circles when a stone is tossed into a pond. In the same way, anything that moves through the air makes waves. These waves

Powerful jet engines such as the XJ-37 helped push airplanes closer to supersonic speeds.

are invisible, but they are real, and if they are strong enough and of the proper frequency, we can hear them.

Because the barrier that apparently existed for airplanes appeared at an airspeed that was the same as the speed of sound waves, it was named "the sound barrier," and many people were convinced that airplanes would never be able to fly any faster.

Scientists and engineers considered the sound barrier a challenge. They knew that aviation progress would come to a stop unless airplanes could fly faster than the speed of sound, and they set out to solve the problem.

During World War II, the German air force had developed a very fast jet fighter, and a rocket plane that had flown 596 miles (960 km) per hour. The British built a jet airplane called the Meteor, and shortly after the war was over, it set a world speed record of 606 miles (976 km) per hour.

The power of jet engines and rockets was pushing airplanes ever closer to the speed of sound, and there were some tragic accidents as pilots explored the unknown and dangerous conditions of very high-speed flight. There were no wind tunnels that could duplicate these conditions, so test pilots had to risk their lives to solve the problems of the sound barrier.

And these were big problems. Flight controls sometimes "froze" at very high speeds, and sometimes the aerodynamic forces became so great that airplanes were torn apart as they approached the speed of sound.

As an airplane moves through the air, it creates waves that move outward in all directions at the speed of sound. At low speeds, an airplane can't ever catch up with its own waves. But when an airplane flies near the speed of sound, it gets closer and closer to the waves it has created.

Suppose an airplane does catch up. Now the waves pile up against each other as they are created, and a

The Meteor (above), built by the British, set a world record at 606 miles per hour in 1945. The Volksjaeger, built by the Germans, could fly at a top speed of 522 miles per hour.

tremendous amount of power is required to push the airplane through its own waves.

Imagine a boat moving slowly across a calm lake. The boat pushes the water ahead of it, forming small waves, and when the speed is increased, the small waves pile up into one larger one. The boat is now pushing along, bow high in the air, but going no faster. If the motor is powerful enough, the boat can push through that wave and speed up rapidly on the other side.

Just as the boat needs more power to get past its own bow wave, an airplane is held back by the sound waves that pile up in front of it at a very high speed. The force holding it back is known as drag, and so it's really a drag barrier—but the original name stuck, and to this day we call it the sound barrier.

Another name—Ernst Mach (pronounced mock)—became part of the language of high-speed flight. Mach was an Austrian physics professor who studied the flight of artillery shells in 1887. He discovered that the strange whistling sound the shells made as they flew overhead was the result of a shock wave—the piling up of air particles ahead of the shells as they reached the speed of sound. Professor Mach developed a convenient numerical scale to describe this speed. He assigned the number 1 to the speed of sound, and decimal numbers for lesser speeds. For example, an artillery shell (or any other object, for that matter) traveling at 80 percent of the speed of sound would be assigned a number of .80, 75 percent would be .75, and so on.

The professor was later honored for his work when his fellow scientists named the numerical scale after him, and the *Mach number* was born. So when the supersonic transport, Concorde, is flying at twice the speed of sound, it's flying at Mach 2—and when you ride a bike at 20 miles (32 km) per hour, you're moving along at the not-so-high speed of Mach .027.

The Mach number makes it easy to describe the actual speed of very fast airplanes, considering that the speed of sound changes at high altitudes. The air becomes much less dense in the upper reaches of the atmosphere, and its temperature gets much lower. This combination results in lowering the speed of sound, but the

Ernst Mach

Mach number continues to indicate an airplane's speed as a percentage of the speed of sound.

For example, an airplane moving 460 miles (741 km) per hour at sea level would be flying at Mach .6. That same 460 miles (741 km) per hour at 40,000 feet (12,200 m) above sea level—where the speed of sound has decreased to about 660 miles (1,063 km) per hour—would produce a Mach number of .7. And that's why pilots who want to fly at high Mach numbers fly at very high altitudes.

The Bell X-1 Rocket Plane

Even before the start of World War II, engineers and designers were aware that high-speed aircraft would probably need to be powered by rocket motors. At the altitudes required for these flights, the air is so thin that air-breathing engines—such as jets—aren't able to produce enough thrust.

The United States' interest in rocket-powered, high-speed flight had lagged behind Germany's, and as a result, the German air force was able to develop the world's first rocket fighter: the Me.163B Komet. This revolutionary airplane was first encountered in the skies over Germany in June 1944, and it took the United States by surprise. Within a matter of months, the U.S. Army Air Corps arranged for Bell Aircraft to build a rocket-powered research plane. The secret project was named MX-524, and the airplane that resulted was to be called the X-1 (X for experimental, and 1 to designate the first in a series of high-speed research vehicles).

The X-1 was intended to explore and, it was hoped, break the sound barrier. But designers had very little information to help them come up with a shape that would do the job. Their research uncovered aerodynamic studies of .50-caliber bullets, which were known to travel smoothly through the air at the speed of sound. And so the fuselage of the new airplane was designed to look like a 31-foot-long (9.5 m) machine-gun bullet. It had a sharp point at the nose, swelling into a fat, chunky midsection, then tapering gradually to the rocket exhaust at the tail.

The experimental Bell X-1 was an important step in the process of refining rocket-powered airplanes in the United States.

To keep the shape smooth and unbroken, there was no bubble canopy over the cockpit, which meant that the pilot would have extremely limited vision straight ahead. But there would be nothing to run into where the X-1 was going . . . visibility was not a primary consideration.

Wing design presented another problem. An airplane's wings generate lift because the upper surfaces are curved slightly, and when the wing is moved through the air, the curvature forces the air to move faster over the top of the wing. This reduces the pressure somewhat and causes the higher pressure underneath to exert a lifting force on the entire airplane.

But at very high speeds, the airflow over the top of the wing speeds up enough to reach the speed of sound before the air flowing around the rest of the plane does. Sound waves pile up on the wing's upper surfaces and become shock waves, which create huge amounts of drag and interference with the flight controls.

The wings for the X-1 would need to be very flat and very thin, but such wings don't do well at low airspeeds—a requirement for safe landing—and so the designers reached a compromise. The X-1's wings were curved just enough to permit landings at a reasonable speed, about 190 miles (306 km) per hour, yet flat

Bell X-1
World's First Supersonic Airplane

1 PITOT TUBE
2 HIGH PRESSURE NITROGEN SPHERES
3 COCKPIT ENTRANCE R.H. SIDE
4 CONTROL STICK
5 HEAD REST
6 YAW ANGLE VANE
7 AILERON TRIM TAB ACTUATOR
8 PILOT CONTROLLABLE AILERON TRIM TAB
9 SPOILERS
10 INSTRUMENT COMPARTMENT
   (RESEARCH EQUIPMENT)
11 WATER ALCOHOL TANK
12 PRESSURE TUBES
13 STABILIZER - MOVEMENT UP 5º DN. 10º
   PILOT CONTROLLED
14 RADIO ANTENNA
15 RUDDER - RIGHT 15º LEFT 15º
16 RUDDER TRIM TAB
17 BALANCE WEIGHTS
18 ROCKET MOTOR 6000# THRUST
19 FLAPS - 60º MOVEMENT
20 AILERONS - TRAVEL 12º UP 12º DN.
21 TAPERED WING SKIN
22 RETRACTABLE MAIN GEAR
23 LIQUID OXYGEN TANK
24 PILOTS COCKPIT (PRESSURIZED)
25 PILOTS SHOULDER HARNESS &
   SAFETY BELT
26 RETRACTABLE NOSE GEAR
27 BATTERY
28 SPOILERS CONTROL
29 RUDDER PEDALS
30 BRAKE CYLINDERS

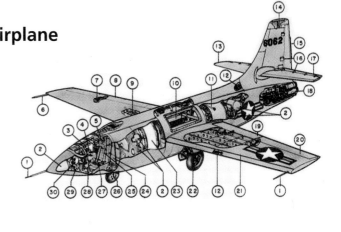

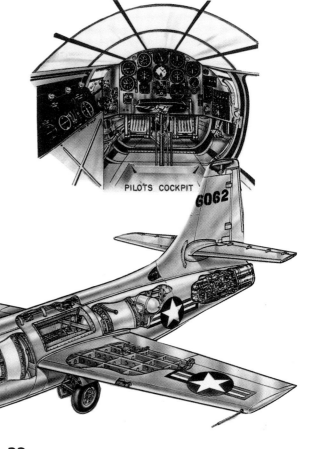

PILOTS COCKPIT

enough and thin enough to delay the formation of shock waves as the airplane approached the speed of sound.

The wings measured 28 feet (8.5 m) from tip to tip, and were designed to support eighteen times the X-1's weight—they were the strongest wings ever built. To help the airplane break cleanly through the shock waves at Mach 1, the leading edges of the wings were very sharp.

All of these aerodynamic "tricks" would be worthless without an engine powerful enough to push the X-1 through the sound barrier, and beyond, to its intended speed of 800 miles (1,288 km) per hour. In 1945 there were no jet engines available that could operate at the altitudes planned for the X-1. A jet engine is an air breather that develops thrust by burning a mixture of air and kerosene and extracting energy as the heated air expands. But at very high altitudes, there simply isn't enough air for a jet to breathe. A rocket engine was the answer.

Rocket engines also rely on burning fuel to produce heat and thrust, but unlike jets, a rocket carries its own "air" in the form of liquid oxygen—a highly concentrated supply of O_2, the chemical element that is required for combustion. Once a rocket motor is ignited, it makes no difference whether it's operating in thick air or thin

The B-29 (below) is shown in flight with the doors of its bomb bays open. A close-up of the bomb bays is shown on the right. After being modified, a B-29 could carry the X-1 attached to its bomb bay.

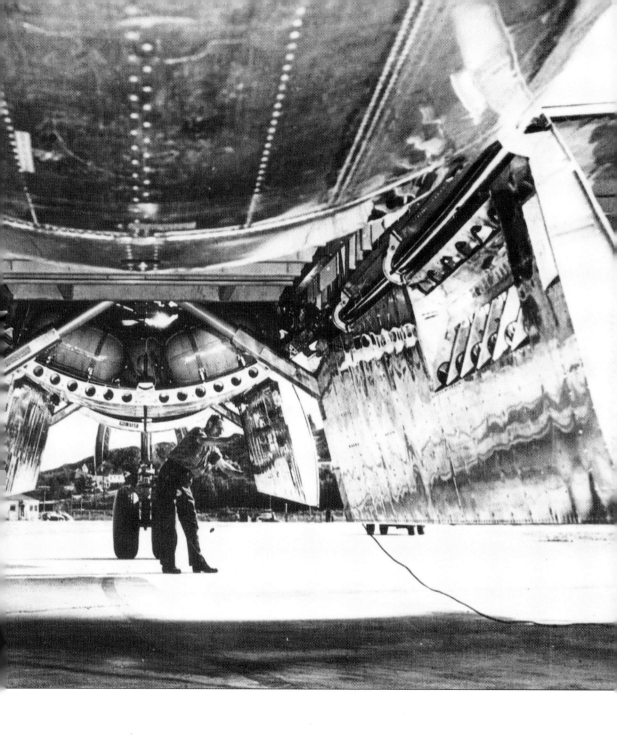

air, or no air at all. The rocket motor would keep on pushing the X-1 until the pilot shut it off, or until all the fuel had been burned.

There are two kinds of rockets: those with solid propellants ("Fourth-of-July rockets," packed with dry chemicals that burn rapidly when ignited), and those in which two or more liquid chemicals are pumped into a combustion chamber and burned. The liquid propellant rocket that was chosen for the X-1 used a mixture of liquid oxygen, alcohol, and water, and the fuel tanks were large enough to provide about nine minutes of thrust at full power.

The X-1's rocket engine was made up of four separate combustion chambers, and the pilot could select one, two, three, or all four chambers. When all four were ignited, the motor produced 6,000 pounds (2,722 kg) of thrust. The engineers calculated that would be enough to push the X-1, which weighed 13,500 pounds (6,124 kg) through the sound barrier.

The very limited fuel supply meant that the X-1 would not be able to take off by itself, climb to 40,000-plus feet (12,200-plus m) and still have enough fuel to power it past the speed of sound. So a B-29—a four-engine bomber—was modified to carry the X-1 in its bomb bay. The plan called for the B-29 to take the rocket ship to 20,000 feet (6,100 m) and drop it, where-upon the pilot would fire the rocket motor and the X-1 would climb the rest of the way by itself.

For landing, the X-1 was fitted with two main wheels, one under each wing, and a single nosewheel directly under the cockpit. The wheels were tucked away in the belly of the X-1 inside the fuselage during the climb, the test run, and the glide back to earth. A mechanism powered by nitrogen gas pressure would extend the wheels before landing.

The Test Location:
Muroc Dry Lake, California

Why in the world would the U.S. Army Air Corps choose such a remote, forbidding site for what would be one of the most significant milestones in aviation?

The answer lies in the geography of the Mojave Desert, north of Los Angeles, and especially the area known as Muroc Dry Lake, a name that seems to contradict itself—a lake is a body of water, not a desert. But each year, when the winter rains come to the high desert, the flat, sandy areas become shallow lakes, just a few inches deep. In the spring, the water evaporates and leaves behind a vast area of smooth, hard sand—the world's greatest natural airfield.

The Army Air Corps began using Muroc Dry Lake for a bombing range in 1931, and Muroc continued to serve as a training base throughout World War II.

The Mojave Desert is the site of Muroc Dry Lake, where the X-1 project began to take shape.

Several landing areas were marked out on the hard sand, and there's now a paved runway 15,000 feet (4,575 m) long that serves as an alternate landing site for space shuttles. The name has changed—it's now

Runway 23 at Edwards Air Force Base in the Mojave Desert is the world's greatest natural airfield.

Edwards Air Force Base in honor of Air Force test pilot Glen Edwards, who was killed in 1948 while testing a new bomber—but the dry lake's physical characteristics are just as attractive as ever to test pilots.

When the X-1 project began to take shape, Muroc Dry Lake was the logical place to set up shop. The long runways gave the B-29 "mother ship" plenty of room for takeoff with the X-1 slung underneath and plenty of room for the X-1 to get stopped after its high-speed landing. In addition, the remote location provided unlimited airspace for the test flights.

Formed eons ago, and continuously improved by the action of wind and water on its hard sand surface, Muroc Dry Lake was the ideal location for the project that would result in the first manned flight beyond the speed of sound.

The Pilot: Captain Charles E. Yeager

No one really knew what might happen to either pilot or airplane on the other side of the sound barrier. A British test pilot, Geoffrey De Havilland, Jr., had flown very close to the speed of sound in September 1946. His airplane was so badly buffeted by the extreme forces it encountered that it broke apart in the air; De Havilland was killed, and no light was shed on the problem of high-speed flight.

Years later, when the United States was preparing for flights into space (where conditions were even more mysterious), scientists trained a group of monkeys and sent them aloft, one at a time, in the first space capsules to make sure there were no hazards that couldn't be overcome by a human pilot.

The X-1 and the sound barrier presented an entirely different set of circumstances. The flights of the early space capsules were ground-controlled from beginning to end—the monkeys were merely along for the ride—

but the X-1 would have to be flown hands-on by a human pilot who could make on-the-spot decisions. On top of that, many scientists and engineers thought the sound barrier was a limit that would never be exceeded. Geoffrey De Havilland's accident was fresh in everyone's mind.

The list of pilots who might have flown the X-1 through the sound barrier included several test pilots who worked for Bell Aircraft.

Test pilot Jack Woolams was the first to fly the X-1.

Jack Woolams, the first pilot to fly the airplane, was at the controls in Florida in January 1946, when the X-1 was put through a series of glide tests. He would probably have continued to fly the X-1, but was killed later that year while practicing for an air race.

Colonel Albert Boyd's 623 mile-per-hour world record was to stand for only a few months.

Alvin M. "Tex" Johnston (left) and copilot R. L. Loesch stand beneath
one of the first tanker-transports.

And there was Chalmers Goodlin, who had flown the X-1 twenty times in 1947. He reached Mach .8, but wanted a five-year, $150,000 contract to continue the program. The Air Force, however, didn't want to pay Goodlin because it could use its own pilots for free. The Air Force also didn't want a civilian to be the first pilot to break the sound barrier.

Another Bell test pilot, Alvin Johnston, flew the X-1 and also felt that the attempt to break the sound barrier was indeed worth a bonus for the pilot who would take the risk. But the company refused the extra pay, and the test program came to a halt.

Colonel Albert Boyd, the Army's chief of flight testing, persuaded the government to let the Air Corps take over the job of trying to break through the sound barrier. He also had a number of aviators from whom to choose—125 of them, to be exact, all very highly qualified test pilots. Colonel Boyd felt he needed someone special for this assignment, and he found what he wanted in the most junior pilot in the group.

Captain Charles Elwood Yeager was only twenty-four years old when he was selected to fly the X-1. He had an outstanding natural talent for flying airplanes, and his experiences as a fighter pilot during World War II had sharpened his skills.

Chuck Yeager was born in 1923 in the tiny town of Myra, West Virginia, the son of a poor farm family. Blessed with remarkable eyesight and an instinct for hunting, he became an expert marksman, a talent that proved to be a great asset in aerial combat. He always saw enemy airplanes sooner than other pilots.

In 1941 the United States was drawn into World War II, and Yeager enlisted in the Army Air Corps. Originally trained as an aircraft mechanic, he soon found his way into flight training and graduated from pilot school in 1943.

Yeager was sent to England and began flying combat missions. His airplane was the Bell P-39 Airacobra, a relatively slow fighter, but his superior vision and hunter's instinct enabled him to shoot down two enemy planes soon after he arrived.

On his ninth combat mission, Yeager's airplane was set afire by enemy bullets, and he was forced to parachute from his burning fighter. He was rescued by friendly French people, who hid him from the Germans, and three months later he was back with his squadron in England. Yeager continued building an outstanding combat record, and after fifty-five more missions, he had accounted for downing ten enemy planes. He was a double ace.

The Bell X-1 was called *Glamorous Glennis* in honor of Chuck Yeager's wife.

Colonel Boyd was well aware of the importance of choosing the right man to fly the X-1. An accident during this important project would be a severe blow to the country's high-speed research program. The X-1 pilot would need to fly with extreme skill and precision, he had to be 100 percent reliable, and he would need to accept without question the high risks of taking an experimental airplane into a realm of flight that was completely unknown.

Yeager was a perfect fit. He was sent to the Bell Aircraft factory to inspect the X-1, and when he returned, he told Colonel Boyd it was the most tremendous airplane he'd ever seen. Yes, he really wanted to fly it. "Okay, Yeager," said the colonel, "it's your ride." And Chuck Yeager began training to become the first human being to fly faster than the speed of sound.

Approaching the Sound Barrier

The test program laid out for the X-1 was designed to take it up to the sound barrier in easy steps, the first of which was a series of gliding flights. The B-29 mother ship would climb to an altitude of 25,000 feet (7,625 m) or so, where Yeager would climb down into the little rocket ship and strap himself into the cockpit. Then the bomber would nose over into a shallow dive, picking up speed, and on a prearranged signal, the X-1 would be dropped.

At this point, Chuck Yeager was flying the world's fastest glider. Between release from the bomber and landing on the dry lake bed, there was time for him to get accustomed to the airplane's sounds and sensations and its response to the flight controls. Landing the X-1, named *Glamorous Glennis* in honor of Yeager's wife, required special skill because of the high speed, and each one of the glide tests gave Yeager an opportunity to get better at landing the little airplane safely.

August 29, 1947, was the date of the first powered flight with Yeager at the controls. The X-1 was loaded with fuel early in the morning, and a half hour after takeoff, the B-29 leveled off 25,000 feet (7,625 m) above the desert.

When the X-1 was dropped for Yeager's first experience with the awesome power of the airplane's rocket motors, it was 3,000 pounds (1,361 kg) heavier than before because of the fuel. On top of that, the B-29 was flying a bit too slowly when the X-1 was dropped. The result was that the plane fell out of the bomb bay, not in a level attitude but with its nose much too high, and it fell 1,000 feet (305 m) before Yeager could get it under complete control.

Then he switched on the first of the four rocket chambers and was slammed back in his seat by the sudden thrust. The X-1 was now in a steep climb; and according to the flight plan, Yeager switched off the first rocket and turned on the second. By the time he had tried all four chambers, the airplane was at 45,000 feet (13,725 m), flying at Mach .7, and still climbing.

At this point, Yeager the test pilot gave in to Yeager the fighter pilot. He had followed the flight plan precisely, lighting one rocket motor at a time, checking temperatures and pressures, and doing all the things

(top) The Bell X-1A, an updated version of the X-1 supersonic plane, is being carried by a B-29 mother ship. (bottom) The X1-A made its first powered flight with an F-86 chase plane close behind.

expected of him. The next thing on the checklist was to dump the remaining fuel and glide down to Muroc Dry Lake for a landing just as in the other test flights.

But Yeager was so thrilled with the performance of the X-1, and so excited about being up so high and flying so fast, that he couldn't resist doing a slow roll. When the airplane was upside down—a condition the designers didn't plan for—the rocket motor quit, then started again as Yeager rolled the X-1 right side up.

The fighter pilot still wasn't satisfied. Yeager shut down the engine, but instead of dumping the rest of the fuel, he pushed the X-1's nose down and started a high-speed dive toward Muroc. At 300 feet (92 m) above the runway and a speed of Mach .8, he did what fighter pilots have done for years—he buzzed the control tower. Opposite the tower, Yeager flicked the switch that turned on all four rocket chambers at the same time, pointed the nose straight up, and climbed to 35,000 feet (10,675 m) at Mach .85. The X-1 was more like a sky-rocket than an airplane.

After landing from this first powered flight, Yeager was in trouble because he had disobeyed orders. The scientists and engineers insisted that the Mach number should be increased only .02 on each flight. They wanted to approach the sound barrier in small steps rather than all at once, taking care of problems as they showed up. So, Yeager the fighter pilot gave in to Yeager the test pilot, and the program proceeded as planned. The X-1 was flown only twice a week, a little faster each time, giving the engineers time to analyze the data and plan the next flight.

The sixth powered flight took place on October 5. At Mach .86, Yeager encountered shock-wave buffeting for the first time. It was like driving on a rough road in a

car with bad shock absorbers, and the flight controls became sluggish. Everyone knew that shock waves would cause problems like this, and the tests continued, but as the speed increased, the control problems became critical. The engineers had predicted that when the X-1 finally reached the speed of sound the nose would try to move up or down, and if the pilot couldn't stop that move-

Captain Charles E. Yeager in an official Air Force portrait

ment with the elevator control, disaster would surely follow. Yeager discovered that at Mach .94, shock waves on the elevator (the moving part of the horizontal tail surface) made it totally useless, so the test program came to a halt until the problem could be solved.

This is what was wrong: the X-1's flight controls were no different from those on most airplanes, which meant that when they were moved, they altered the airflow and changed the amount of lift produced by the wings and tail. The pilot controlled pitch (nose up or down) with the elevators, bank (wings rolling left or right) with the ailerons, and yaw (nose moving left or right) with the rudder. In the case of the elevator, shock waves generated by the horizontal stabilizer (the non-moving part of the tail) disturbed the airflow so badly at high speeds that the elevator couldn't do its job.

The problem was overcome by making the horizontal stabilizer movable. Using a switch in the cockpit, Yeager could now change the angle at which the stabilizer moved through the air. From then on, whenever the elevator became ineffective, a slight change in the stabilizer setting would restore control, and Yeager could push on to higher speeds.

The X-1 was accompanied on each flight by two chase planes. These were Lockheed P-80s, the United

LOCKHEE

The pilot of a chase plane such as the one shown here, provided invaluable aid during early supersonic test flights.

States' first jet fighters, but they couldn't begin to keep up with the X-1 during the high-speed portions of the flights. The chase pilots were there to check the condition of the X-1 after it was released from the B-29, and to offer help, if Yeager needed it, during the glide back to earth and the landing on the dry lake.

On one of the early powered flights, when it appeared that the sound barrier was almost within reach, something completely unexpected took place. It would have been a disaster but for the skill of Chuck Yeager and one of the chase pilots, Dick Frost. At the end of the flight, when the X-1 had reached Mach .96 at 43,000 feet (13,115 m), the windshield frosted over completely, making it impossible for Yeager to see anything outside. He was truly flying blind.

Yeager had plenty of experience in "blind flying"— using only the instruments on the panel in front of him to control the airplane—but the X-1 had no navigation equipment, and the fact that it was now a glider meant that he would have only one chance for a safe landing. The chase pilot would have to guide him all the way to the ground.

Frost was a highly experienced pilot who had been through the same training and knew the X-1 and its characteristics as well as Yeager. He moved into position very close to the X-1, then flew the normal approach, talking to Yeager on the radio and telling him when to turn, when to descend, when to lower the landing gear. As the two airplanes approached the landing area on the dry lake, Frost directed Yeager through several heading changes to get lined up with the runway.

Keeping his airplane in position just a few feet from the X-1's wingtip, Frost flew right down to the ground and landed alongside Yeager. Muroc Dry Lake's runway, 5 miles (8 km) wide and 8 miles (13 km) long, had saved another life and a valuable research vehicle. The X-1 test program continued toward the speed of sound.

The Barrier Is Broken

Tuesday morning, October 14, 1947. Dawn on the desert, and the X-1 is being fueled for the day's flights. The liquid oxygen—at a temperature of –297°F (–183°C)!—makes a loud, screaming noise as it is transferred from storage tanks to the fuel system of the X-1. There are only a few ground-crew members on hand, and as the sun comes up, Chuck Yeager arrives to check over the X-1 before it is loaded into the bomb bay of the mother ship.

This day appears to be starting off just like any other day in the test program, except for something that is known to only Yeager and his crew chief, Jack Ridley. Two days ago while riding horseback, Yeager had been thrown and had broken two ribs. The doctor insisted that Yeager take it easy for a couple of weeks— give the broken bones a chance to heal. But Chuck Yeager was not one to let something like that stand in the way of completing the assignment.

(left) The X-1 broke through the sound barrier while flying about 700 miles per hour on October 14, 1947. (below) Chuck Yeager was the first person to fly faster than the speed of sound.

He knew that he could stand the pain, but he also knew that he needed a strong right arm to close and lock the hatch through which he entered the X-1, and his right arm was practically useless. Ridley solved the problem with a sawed-off broomstick that gave Yeager enough leverage to reach over and lock the hatch with his left hand. Without Jack Ridley's ingenuity and that 9-inch (23-cm) piece of wood, a milestone in aviation might not have been reached, at least not on October 14, 1947.

Still hurting but anxious to get on with the job, Yeager climbed aboard the B-29. At 7,000 feet (2,135 m), he climbed down the ladder and settled into the X-1 cockpit. Ridley handed him the broomstick, Yeager got the door closed and locked, and signaled that he was ready to go.

The objective for this flight was to push the X-1 to Mach .97, but Yeager was growing impatient with the scientists' one-step-at-a-time progress toward the sound barrier. He felt that he and the airplane could take whatever forces might be encountered at the speed of sound, and if the X-1 could break through the barrier, the only way to find out would be to do it.

When the B-29 reached 26,000 feet (7,930 m) its pilot started a shallow dive to pick up speed for the drop, and at 20,000 feet (6,100 m) he released the X-1. When it fell free, at the same speed as the mother ship, the X-1 wallowed in a near stall, its tiny wings unable

General Hoyt S. Vandenberg, Army Air Forces chief, presents the Mackay Trophy for the most meritorious flight of 1947 to Captain Charles Yeager.

to provide much lift at this low airspeed. Yeager got the airplane under control after falling 500 feet (153 m), and then he fired all four rockets, one right after the other.

The X-1 climbed at Mach .88, sailed through 36,000 feet (10,980 m), where Yeager shut down two of the chambers to save fuel, and the climb continued at Mach .92. When he leveled the X-1 at 42,000 feet (12,810 m), 30 percent of the fuel remained, so Yeager fired the third rocket chamber again. The airspeed immediately jumped to Mach .96—and he noticed that as the airplane moved faster, the ride got smoother.

Then it happened. The needle on the Mach indicator gauge started to move back and forth, went up to Mach .965, then went clear off the scale. Without a bump, as smooth as glass, the X-1 had gone supersonic! Chuck Yeager had become the first human being to fly faster than the speed of sound.

The indicator in the X-1 didn't register beyond Mach 1, but the data showed that the little orange airplane had reached Mach 1.06—about 700 miles (1,127 km) per hour. Engineers in a tracking van miles away reported hearing the thunder of Yeager's sonic boom, and everyone at Muroc Dry Lake knew they had a hero in their midst.

President Harry Truman awards the Collier Air Trophy, aviation's highest honor, to Captain Charles Yeager in December 1948.

The X-1 is now on display in the National Air and Space Museum of the Smithsonian Institution in Washington, D.C.

Chuck Yeager flew the X-1 on forty missions after the first supersonic flight. He eventually reached a speed of 1,000 miles (1,600 km) per hour and an altitude of more than 70,000 feet (21,350 m). But after breaking the sound barrier on October 14, 1947, he didn't feel much like a hero. He felt very tired, his right side hurt, and he wanted nothing more than to go home and nurse his aching ribs.

Chuck Yeager retired with the rank of brigadier general after flying 10,000 hours in military aircraft.

Facts, Figures, Important Dates

The Pilot: Charles Elwood Yeager

Born: February 13, 1923, in Myra, West Virginia

After completing research flights in the Bell X-1, Chuck Yeager remained at Edwards Air Force Base as a test pilot until 1954. He then resumed his career as a fighter pilot, served in combat in Vietnam, and retired as a brigadier general in 1975. He had flown 10,000 hours in 180 different types of military aircraft. Yeager then took a job as a test pilot for a manufacturer of high-performance fighters.

In recognition of his feat in breaking the sound barrier, Chuck Yeager was awarded the Medal of Honor and was enshrined in the Aviation Hall of Fame in Dayton, Ohio.

The Airplane: The Bell X-1 (*Glamorous Glennis,* named for Yeager's wife)

The X-1 was a single-seat, rocket-propelled monoplane, designed solely for supersonic research. Several of these airplanes were built during the research program. All but two were destroyed in accidents. One is on display at Edwards Air Force Base, the other—the first airplane to fly faster than the speed of sound—is a permanent exhibit in the National Air and Space Museum, in Washington, D.C.

Specifications:

Weight—fully loaded, 13,400 pounds (6,078 kg); fuel weight—8,177 pounds (3,709 kg)

Length—31 feet (9.5 m)

Wingspan—28 feet (8.5 m)

Height—10 feet, 10.2 inches (3.3 m)

Power plant—Four rocket chambers burning alcohol and liquid oxygen, total thrust 6,000 pounds (2,722 kg)

First flight—Early 1946 at Orlando, Florida (unpowered)

First powered fight—December 9, 1946, at Muroc Dry Lake

First powered takeoff—January 5, 1949, at Muroc Dry Lake

For Further Reading

Gaffney, Timothy R. *Voyager, Chuck Yeager: First Man to Fly Faster Than Sound.* Chicago: Childrens Press, 1986.

Jefferies, David. *Supersonic Flight.* New York: Franklin Watts, 1988.

Levinson, Nancy Smiler. *Chuck Yeager: The Man Who Broke the Sound Barrier.* New York: Walker, 1988.

Rosenblum, Robert A. *Aviators.* New York: Facts on File, 1992.

Index

About the Author

Richard L. Taylor is an associate professor emeritus in the Department of Aviation at Ohio State University, having retired in 1988 after twenty-two years as an aviation educator. At retirement, he was the Director of Flight Operations and Training, with responsibility for all flight training and university air transportation. He holds two degrees from Ohio State University: a B.S. in agriculture and an M.A. in journalism.

His first aviation book, *Instrument Flying*, was published in 1972, and continues in its third edition as one of the best-sellers in popular aviation literature. Since then, he has written five more books for pilots, and hundreds of articles and columns for aviation magazines.

Taylor began his aviation career in 1955 when he entered U.S. Air Force pilot training, and after four years on active duty continued his military activity as a reservist until retirement as a major and command pilot in 1979.

Still active as a pilot and accident investigator, as well as a writer, Taylor flies frequently for business and pleasure. His books for Franklin Watts include *First Flight*, *The First Solo Flight Around the World*, *The First Flight Across the United States*, and *The First Supersonic Flight*. He and his wife live in Dublin, a suburb of Columbus, Ohio.

3

7268